UPPER

Multiple-Choice Comprehension

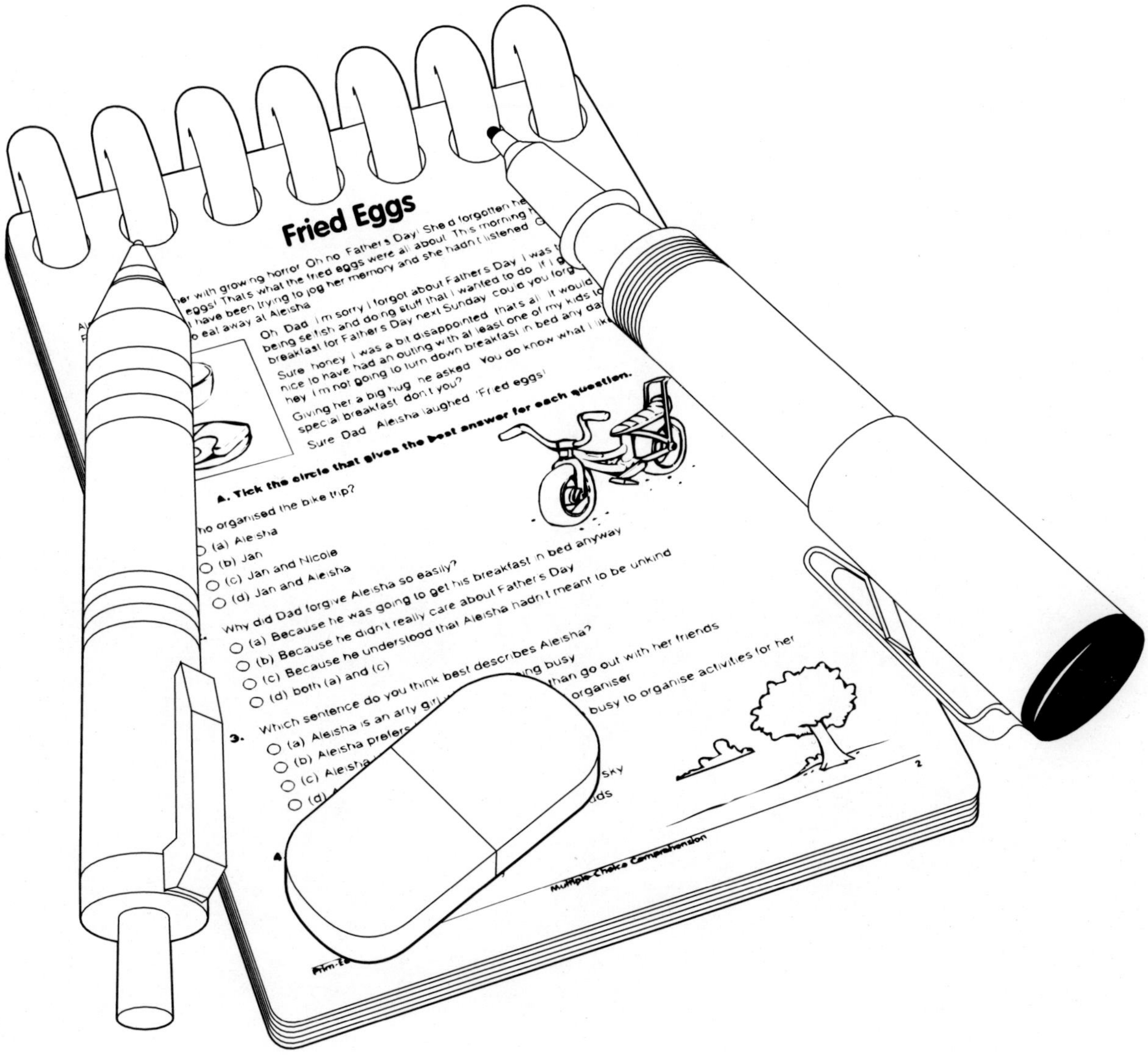

Written by Carole Booth
Published by Prim-Ed Publishing

UK–2083
REV05/02

39/4

MULTIPLE CHOICE COMPREHENSION *(Upper)*

First published in 1998 by Curriculum Concepts
Revised and reprinted under licence in 2000 by Prim-Ed Publishing

ISBN 978-1-86400-568-4
PR–2083

Other titles available in this series:

MULTIPLE CHOICE COMPREHENSION *(Lower)*
MULTIPLE CHOICE COMPREHENSION *(Middle)*

'rim-Ed Publishing
/arshmeadows
lew Ross
:o. Wexford

/www.prim-ed.com

ıternet websites

some cases, websites or specific URLs may be recommended. While these are checked and rechecked at the time of publication, e publisher has no control over any subsequent changes which may be made to webpages. It is *strongly* recommended that the class acher checks *all* URLs before allowing pupils to access them.

Foreword

Multiple-Choice Comprehension is a three-book series featuring a collection of original fiction stories. The high-interest stories feature strong main characters and involving plots.

The follow-up comprehension activities are divided into two sections:

Section A – multiple-choice questions requiring literal, interpretative and evaluative/appreciative answers.

Section B – varied activities designed to encourage pupils to reflect on the text, including true/false, word study, dictionary usage and sequencing.

Multiple-Choice Comprehension is a comprehensive comprehension series which also includes teachers notes, answers and English national curriculum links.

The three books in this series are:

Multiple Choice Comprehension – Lower *(Key Stage One)*
Multiple-Choice Comprehension – Middle (*Key Stage Two – Years 3 and 4*)
Multiple-Choice Comprehension – Upper (*Key Stage Two – Years 5 and 6*)

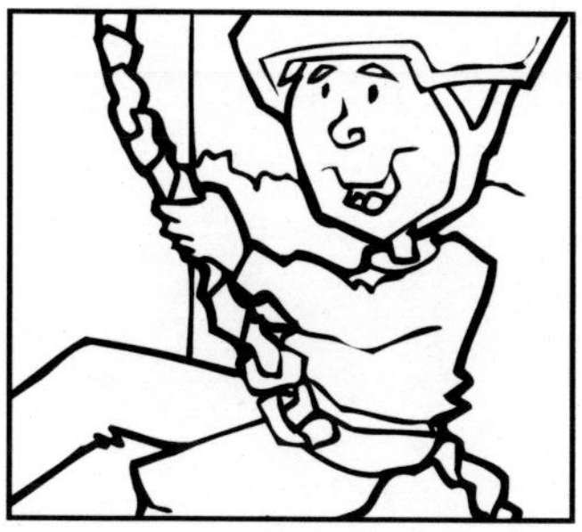

Contents

Teachers Notes

Multiple-Choice Comprehension – Upper consists of nine original fiction stories for upper primary pupils. Each story and its corresponding activities take up three to four pages and cover the following:

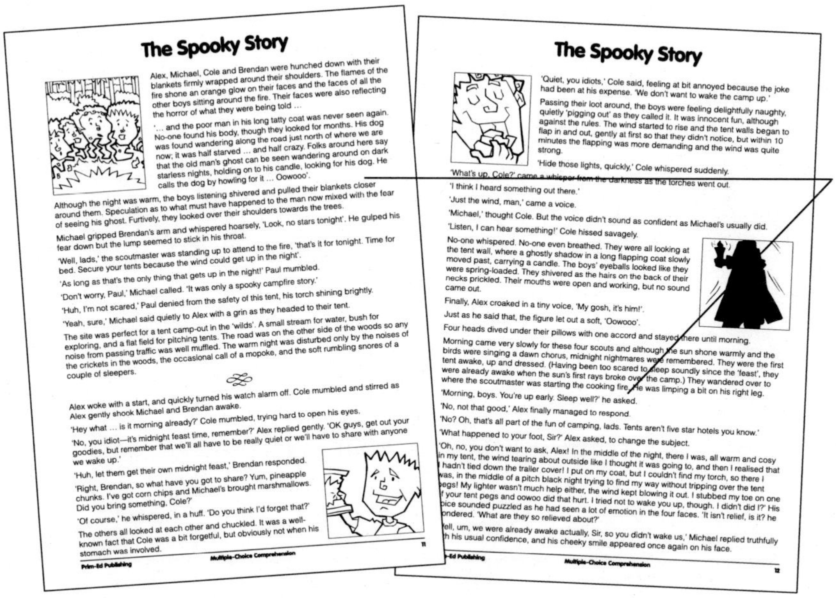
The Spooky Story

Alex, Michael, Cole and Brendan were hunched down with their blankets firmly wrapped around their shoulders. The flames of the fire shone an orange glow on their faces and the faces of all the other boys sitting around the fire. Their faces were also reflecting the horror of what they were being told …

'… and the poor man in his long tatty coat was never seen again. No-one found his body, though they looked for months. His dog was found wandering along the road just north of where we are now; it was half starved … and half crazy. Folks around here say that the old man's ghost can be seen wandering around on dark starless nights, holding on to his candle, looking for his dog. He calls the dog by howling for it … Oowooo'.

Although the night was warm, the boys listening shivered and pulled their blankets closer around them. Speculation as to what must have happened to the man now mixed with the fear of seeing his ghost. Furtively, they looked over their shoulders towards the trees.

Michael gripped Brendan's arm and whispered hoarsely, 'Look, no stars tonight'. He gulped his fear down but the lump seemed to stick in his throat.

'Well, lads,' the scoutmaster was standing up to attend to the fire, 'that's it for tonight. Time for bed. Secure your tents because the wind could get up in the night'.

'As long as that's the only thing that gets up in the night!' Paul mumbled.

'Don't worry, Paul,' Michael called. 'It was only a spooky campfire story.'

'Huh, I'm not scared,' Paul denied from the safety of this tent, his torch shining brightly.

'Yeah, sure,' Michael said quietly to Alex with a grin as they headed to their tent.

The site was perfect for a tent camp-out in the 'wilds'. A small stream for water, bush for exploring, and a flat field for pitching tents. The road was on the other side of the woods so any noise from passing traffic was well muffled. The warm night was disturbed only by the noises of the crickets in the woods, the occasional call of a mopoke, and the soft rumbling snores of a couple of sleepers.

Alex woke with a start, and quickly turned his watch alarm off. Cole mumbled and stirred as Alex gently shook Michael and Brendan awake.

'Hey what … is it morning already?' Cole mumbled, trying hard to open his eyes.

'No, you idiot—it's midnight feast time, remember?' Alex replied gently. 'OK guys, get out your goodies, but remember that we'll all have to be really quiet or we'll have to share with anyone we wake up.'

'Huh, let them get their own midnight feast,' Brendan responded.

'Right, Brendan, so what have you got to share? Yum, pineapple chunks. I've got corn chips and Michael's brought marshmallows. Did you bring something, Cole?'

'Of course,' he whispered, in a huff. 'Do you think I'd forget that?'

The others all looked at each other and chuckled. It was a well-known fact that Cole was a bit forgetful, but obviously not when his stomach was involved.

Prim-Ed Publishing Multiple-Choice Comprehension 11

The Spooky Story

'Quiet, you idiots,' Cole said, feeling at bit annoyed because the joke had been at his expense. 'We don't want to wake the camp up.'

Passing their loot around, the boys were feeling delightfully naughty, quietly 'pigging out' as they called it. It was innocent fun, although against the rules. The wind started to rise and the tent walls began to flap in and out, gently at first so that they didn't notice, but within 10 minutes the flapping was more demanding and the wind was quite strong.

'Hide those lights, quickly,' Cole whispered suddenly.

'What's up, Cole?' came a whisper from the darkness as the torches went out.

'I think I heard something out there.'

'Just the wind, man,' came a voice.

'Michael,' thought Cole. But the voice didn't sound as confident as Michael's usually did.

'Listen, I can hear something!' Cole hissed savagely.

No-one whispered. No-one even breathed. They were all looking at the tent wall, where a ghostly shadow in a long flapping coat slowly moved past, carrying a candle. The boys' eyeballs looked like they were spring-loaded. They shivered as the hairs on the back of their necks prickled. Their mouths were open and working, but no sound came out.

Finally, Alex croaked in a tiny voice, 'My gosh, it's him!'.

Just as he said that, the figure let out a soft, 'Oowooo'.

Four heads dived under their pillows with one accord and stayed there until morning.

Morning came very slowly for these four scouts and although the sun shone warmly and the birds were singing a dawn chorus, midnight nightmares were remembered. They were the first tent awake, up and dressed. (Having been too scared to sleep soundly since the 'feast', they were already awake when the sun's first rays broke over the camp.) They wandered over to where the scoutmaster was starting the cooking fire. He was limping a bit on his right leg.

'Morning, boys. You're up early. Sleep well?' he asked.

'No, not that good,' Alex finally managed to respond.

'No? Oh, that's all part of the fun of camping, lads. Tents aren't five star hotels you know.'

'What happened to your foot, Sir?' Alex asked, to change the subject.

'Oh, no, you don't want to ask, Alex! In the middle of the night, there I was, all warm and cosy in my tent, the wind tearing about outside like I thought it was going to, and then I realised that I hadn't tied down the trailer cover! I put on my coat, but I couldn't find my torch, so there I was, in the middle of a pitch black night trying to find my way without tripping over the tent pegs! My lighter wasn't much help either, the wind kept blowing it out. I stubbed my toe on one of your tent pegs and oowoo did that hurt. I tried not to wake you up, though. I didn't do it?' His voice sounded puzzled as he had seen a lot of emotion in the four faces. 'It isn't relief, is it? He pondered. 'What are they so relieved about?'

'Well, um, we were already awake actually, Sir, so you didn't wake us,' Michael replied truthfully with his usual confidence, and his cheeky smile appeared once again on his face.

Prim-Ed Publishing Multiple-Choice Comprehension 12

Page 1–3 contains the story. All stories use high-interest themes relevant to the upper primary age group. Strong main characters and involving plots are featured.

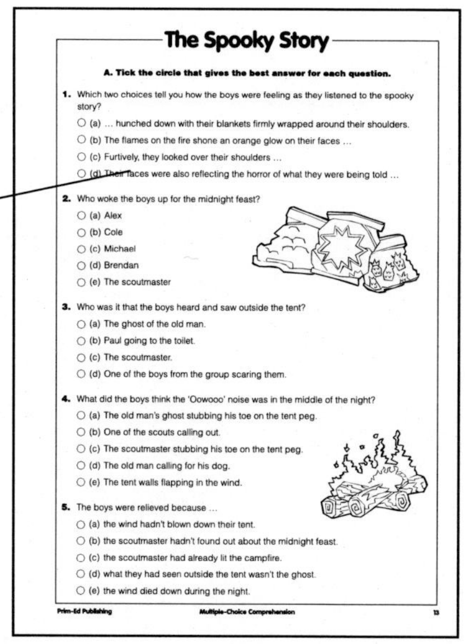
The Spooky Story

A. Tick the circle that gives the best answer for each question.

1. Which two choices tell you how the boys were feeling as they listened to the spooky story?
   - (a) … hunched down with their blankets firmly wrapped around their shoulders.
   - (b) The flames on the fire shone an orange glow on their faces …
   - (c) Furtively, they looked over their shoulders …
   - (d) Their faces were also reflecting the horror of what they were being told …
2. Who woke the boys up for the midnight feast?
   - (a) Alex
   - (b) Cole
   - (c) Michael
   - (d) Brendan
   - (e) The scoutmaster
3. Who was it that the boys heard and saw outside the tent?
   - (a) The ghost of the old man.
   - (b) Paul going to the toilet.
   - (c) The scoutmaster.
   - (d) One of the boys from the group scaring them.
4. What did the boys think the 'Oowooo' noise was in the middle of the night?
   - (a) The old man's ghost stubbing his toe on the tent peg.
   - (b) One of the scouts calling out.
   - (c) The scoutmaster stubbing his toe on the tent peg.
   - (d) The old man calling for his dog.
   - (e) The tent walls flapping in the wind.
5. The boys were relieved because …
   - (a) the wind hadn't blown down their tent.
   - (b) the scoutmaster hadn't found out about the midnight feast.
   - (c) the scoutmaster had already lit the campfire.
   - (d) what they had seen outside the tent wasn't the ghost.
   - (e) the wind died down during the night.

Prim-Ed Publishing Multiple-Choice Comprehension 13

Page 2–3 contains multiple-choice comprehension questions, focusing on characters, plot and word study. Literal, interpretative and evaluative/ appreciative answers are required.

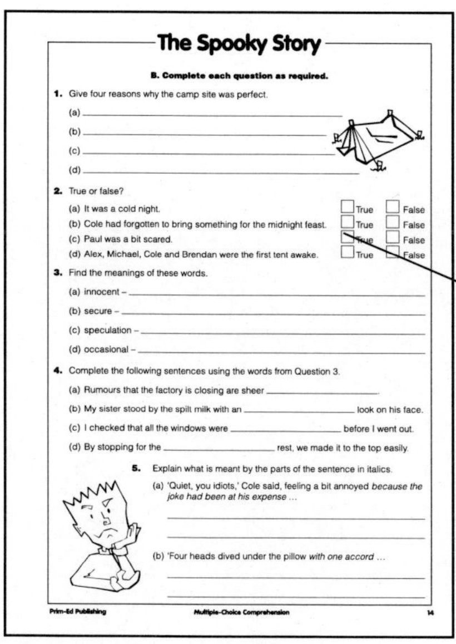
The Spooky Story

B. Complete each question as required.

1. Give four reasons why the camp site was perfect.
   (a) ____
   (b) ____
   (c) ____
   (d) ____
2. True or false?
   (a) It was a cold night. True False
   (b) Cole had forgotten to bring something for the midnight feast. True False
   (c) Paul was a bit scared. True False
   (d) Alex, Michael, Cole and Brendan were the first tent awake. True False
3. Find the meanings of these words.
   (a) innocent – ____
   (b) secure – ____
   (c) speculation – ____
   (d) occasional – ____
4. Complete the following sentences using the words from Question 3.
   (a) Rumours that the factory is closing are sheer ____
   (b) My sister stood by the spilt milk with an ____ look on his face.
   (c) I checked that all the windows were ____ before I went out.
   (d) By stopping for the ____ rest, we made it to the top easily.
5. Explain what is meant by the parts of the sentence in italics.
   (a) 'Quiet, you idiots,' Cole said, feeling a bit annoyed *because the joke had been at his expense …*
   (b) 'Four heads dived under the pillow *with one accord …*

Prim-Ed Publishing Multiple-Choice Comprehension 14

Page 4 uses a variety of activities designed to make pupils reflect further upon the text. Activities include true/ false, word study and sequencing.

Further Ideas

Story themes could be used as a springboard for creative writing

Group discussion of multiple-choice alternatives

Character studies

Multiple-Choice Comprehension Curriculum Links

Upper	Two	Reading	2.a	use inference and deduction
			2.b	look for meanings beyond the literal
			2.c	make connections between different parts of the text
			3.a	scan texts to find information
			3.c	obtain specific information through detailed reading
			3.f	distinguish between fact and opinion
			4.g	express preferences and support their views with reference to texts
			4.h	respond imaginatively, drawing on the whole text
		Writing	3	use punctuation marks correctly in their writing
			7.a	understand word classes and grammatical functions of words, including nouns, verbs and adjectives
			9.a	imagine and explore feelings and ideas in writing
			9.d	review and comment on what has been read

Fried Eggs

Fried eggs! Fried eggs? What on earth have fried eggs got to do with anything? Why should they pop into her mind now, just as she woke up? Aleisha didn't have a clue.

Getting dressed quickly, she ran downstairs. No-one else was up. Her big brother, Joel, was away for the weekend. 'Going fishing,' he'd said. Well, she wasn't going to laze the day away. She had heaps of great things to do. First, grab breakfast, then pack a picnic lunch.

The gang were meeting up at the corner shop, so that anyone who needed to buy something for lunch (or just to munch on) could. Looking out of the kitchen window, Aleisha saw the sun shining in the blue sky … and not a cloud to be seen. It must be nearly 9.30 by now … yes, it was 9.20. Better get going.

Still no sign of her parents. 'Boy, some people are plain lazy on a beautiful Sunday morning, aren't they? Oh well, better go and say goodbye in case they've forgotten my arrangements for the day,' she thought.

'Bye, Mum, bye, Dad. I'm off now for our bike ride—we're going skating afterwards and then we'll be at Jessica's house, so I'm not sure when I'll get home. See you later!' she shouted as she dashed out the door.

'Hello' and 'Hi' came from the group of girls gathered outside the shop as Aleisha rode up.

'Well, if everyone's got their lunch and munchies, we can get started,' Jan suggested as she buckled her helmet back on.

The ride was through a lovely part of the countryside. Trees lined the country road in their autumn colours. Birds sang as they passed and even a lone harrier hawk glided high above them in the cloudless sky. Aleisha smiled to herself. What a day! What a neat day! It was a good thing she'd organised this outing with her friends today; she'd hate a day like this to go to waste.

They stopped for lunch at a picnic table under a tree by the river. Nicole had even thought to bring a plastic tablecloth.

'It covers up the bird poo!' she said with a grin.

It was surprising how six leg-weary girls could find enough energy to put on skates after their bike ride but they did—and boy, they had some fun. They ended up having races and contests against each other. Even the odd bruise on various parts of her anatomy couldn't detract from Aleisha's enjoyment. She liked skating. She'd been to skating lessons when she was younger and liked to practise when she could.

Aleisha arrived home around 4.30 and wandered into the kitchen.

'Oh, hi, Mum, Dad. Gee, I had a great day today, we had a ball! What did you guys do all day?'

'Well …' her mother answered. 'I had a lie-in this morning to start with, because I'd been up late last night working and Dad had a lie-in this morning because he was hoping someone would think to bring him breakfast in bed for his birthday.'

Fried Eggs

Aleisha looked at her with growing horror. Oh no, she'd forgotten her dad's birthday. Fried eggs! That's what the fried eggs were all about. This morning her subconscious must have been trying to jog her memory and she hadn't listened. Guilt with a capital 'G' began to eat away at Aleisha.

'Oh, Dad, I'm sorry I forgot about your birthday. I was too busy being selfish and doing stuff that I wanted to do. If I make you breakfast next Sunday, could you forgive me?'

'Sure, honey. I was a bit disappointed, that's all. It would've been nice to have had an outing with at least one of my kids today. But hey, I'm not going to turn down breakfast in bed any day!'

Giving her a big hug, he asked, 'You do know what I like for my special breakfast, don't you?'

'Sure, Dad,' Aleisha laughed. 'Fried eggs!'

A. Tick the circle that gives the best answer for each question.

1. Who organised the bike trip?

- ○ (a) Aleisha
- ○ (b) Jan
- ○ (c) Jan + Nicole
- ○ (d) Jan + Aleisha

2. Why did Dad forgive Aleisha so easily?

- ○ (a) Because he was going to get his breakfast in bed anyway.
- ○ (b) Because he didn't really care about his birthday.
- ○ (c) Because he understood that Aleisha hadn't meant to be unkind.
- ○ (d) both (a) and (c).

3. Which sentence do you think best describes Aleisha?

- ○ (a) Aleisha is an arty girl who likes being busy.
- ○ (b) Aleisha prefers to laze around than go out with her friends.
- ○ (c) Aleisha likes being busy and is a good organiser.
- ○ (d) Aleisha enjoys outdoor sports and is too busy to organise activities for her friends.

4. What sort of day was it?

- ○ (a) a sunny, autumn day with a clear blue sky
- ○ (b) a sunny, autumn day with a few clouds
- ○ (c) a showery summer's day
- ○ (d) a cloudy, wintry day

Fried Eggs

B. Complete each question as required.

1. Order the sentences.

- 2 (a) The girls met at the shop.
- 4 (b) Dad and Mum told Aleisha about their day.
- 3 (c) The girls went skating.
- 5 (d) Aleisha realised it was her dad's birthday.
- 1 (e) Aleisha had breakfast and then packed her lunch.

2. Complete the sentences.

(a) Aleisha's brother Joel had gone fishing for the weekend.

(b) Nicole spread out a tablecloth made of plastic.

(c) Aleisha had taken skating lessons when she was younger.

(d) Dad liked fried eggs for a special breakfast.

3. Why did Aleisha feel guilty?

She forgot about her dads birthday and was too busy thinking about herself

4. Find the meaning of:

(a) subconscious – ______________________

(b) clue – ______________________

(c) anatomy – ______________________

(d) detract – ______________________

5. Design a menu for a special breakfast for your dad for Father's Day.

Daydreamer

'The function of the brain is to … Lynda!' Mr Armstrong glared at Lynda. 'Stop daydreaming!'

'Huh, pardon, Sir?' Lynda was jolted back to reality rather suddenly when her name was called. 'Drat!' she thought. 'Caught daydreaming in class again.'

'I think you had better stay after school today and study your science book, Lynda. Just to make sure you do know what we've been learning today.'

Lynda groaned inwardly. Why couldn't she just stop daydreaming? It was always getting her into trouble. Once she had tried really hard to stop, but it didn't seem to work. Every time the teacher talked about something she didn't understand or wasn't interested in, her mind started to wander. It seemed to have a will of its own, and she quite happily travelled with it to wherever it took her.

She had been in a beautiful valley, where a river tumbled over rocks on its way to the sea, a gentle breeze ruffled the long grass and a lone eagle glided high in the air. No-one else was around. It was so clear and peaceful that Lynda had thought she was really there … until the teacher had called her back. She really loved those magical places that her mind took her to, but it sure got her into trouble at school.

School was difficult for Lynda. Reading was a struggle and maths was terrifying! She was good at some things like drama, music and poetry, and she was great at art. But it seemed to her that nobody thought these things counted. They weren't the sort of things that helped you get a job when you left school. No-one had actually said that to her, but she knew that's what they all thought.

Lynda smiled a secret little smile to herself as she remembered. It goes to show that although adults were mostly right about things, sometimes they just didn't know what it was that made an individual different and special from everyone else.

The cameras flashed, and people were talking. A photographer asked her to move next to one of the paintings so he could get a good photo. She didn't mind, it was good publicity to have photos of herself and her paintings in newspapers and magazines.

From the crowd of reporters and photographers, a young woman pushed her way through, microphone in hand, and asked, 'Miss Johnson, can you remember what started you off on your art career?' Now the secret smile spread across Lynda's face, a secret smile no longer.

'Yes, I can remember easily. Look behind you at that painting.'

Turning, the reporter could now see the painting that had been hidden by journalists. She looked in amazement at the magical qualities of beauty and the peace of a lovely valley with a lazy river flowing through the tall grass, and a lone eagle gliding high in the air. She hardly heard Miss Johnson saying 'You see, I daydreamed that at school. Daydreaming was one thing I was really good at, that and art. So I concentrated on what I was really good at and what I enjoyed. And I still enjoy daydreaming. It's where I get the inspiration for my paintings.'

Daydreamer

A. Tick the circle that gives the best answer for each question.

1. At school Lynda was good at …

- (a) reading poetry, music, art
- (b) poetry, maths, music, drama
- (c) poetry, art, drama, music
- (d) reading poetry, art, drama, music

2. Choose the statement you think is most correct.

- (a) Lynda was a creative person and enjoyed drama, music, poetry and art.
- (b) Lynda was lazy and wasn't good at any subject.
- (c) Lynda was good in all subject areas but didn't work hard.
- (d) Lynda was good at art but didn't work at it because it wouldn't help her get a job.
- (e) Lynda was especially good at daydreaming.

3. What started Lynda off on her art career?

- (a) Her art teacher set up an exhibition for her.
- (b) She concentrated on what she was really good at.
- (c) She did well at art at school.
- (d) She got a lucky break.

4. What does 'glared' in the first sentence mean?

- (a) shone brightly
- (b) looked fierce
- (c) frowned
- (d) stared
- (e) laughed

5. Why do you think Lynda daydreamed at school?

- (a) She liked daydreaming.
- (b) She didn't like science.
- (c) She was good at daydreaming.
- (d) She daydreamed when she didn't understand something.

Daydreamer

B. Complete each question as required.

1. True or False?

(a) It was good publicity to have her picture in the newspaper.	☒ True	☐ False
(b) Mr Armstrong did not punish Lynda.	☐ True	☒ False
(c) Lynda had tried to stop daydreaming.	☒ True	☐ False
(d) Daydreaming helped Lynda with her painting.	☒ True	☐ False
(e) Mr Armstrong was Lynda's Maths teacher.	☐ True	☒ False

2. Draw the picture to match Lynda's daydream and her final painting.

3. Explain the meaning of these sentences.

(a) '… jolted back to reality …' woke up suddenly

(b) 'It seemed to have a will of its own …' ______________________

4. It seemed to Lynda that nobody thought art, music, drama and poetry were important because they didn't help you get a job. What are your thoughts on this comment?

____

____

____

____

5. List all the types of jobs you can think of which require skill in the subjects in Question 4.

____

____

Freedom for What?

Michael glanced at the clock on the wall. 'Thank goodness,' he thought, 'it's five to three'. He'd been watching that clock for the last hour. The time seemed to have dragged all day.

'Thank goodness it's Friday,' Brendan whispered from behind him.

Michael grinned back, 'Yeah'.

'See you at four, right, Michael?'

'Yeah,' Michael replied, starting to hurriedly pack his books away just as the bell rang.

It was four minutes to four when he arrived to meet 'the gang' at the park. They were all in high spirits because Friday meant 'freedom' for two whole days.

'Well, so what are we gonna do then?' asked Cole from where he stood with his bike.

They all looked at each other, shrugging their shoulders.

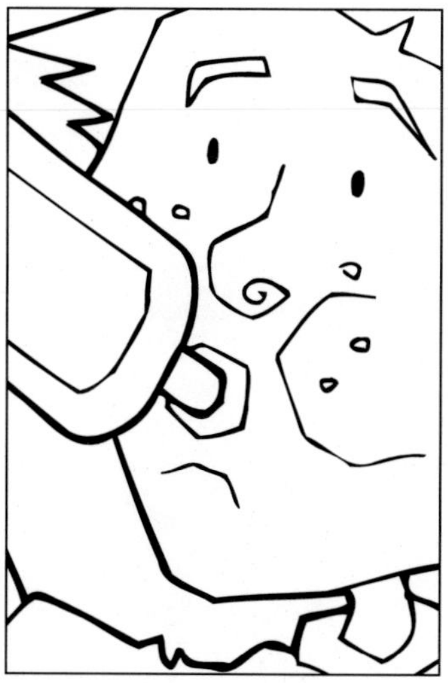

'I know, let's have bike races … to the top of the hill and back,' Brendan suggested.

This kept them occupied for the next hour until finally they dumped their bikes down and sprawled on the grass.

'Man, I'm beat,' Michael said after taking a big long swig from his bike drink bottle.

'Wish my bike had a drink carrier. Though I'd probably forget to put drink in it!' laughed Cole.

The others laughed and teased him a bit. (Cole was known to be a bit forgetful, especially if it suited him to forget, like when his mum gave him a chore to do.)

'Well,' said Michael, rolling over on the grass, 'what can we do now?' Silence followed.

Finally Cole mumbled, 'Yeah, what can we do now? There's nothing to do in this place. It's totally boring. Wish we lived in the city,' he added wistfully. Another silence followed, as each boy considered this.

'You know, guys,' Alex started speaking in a quiet, thoughtful voice, 'I'm considering joining the Scouts'. The reaction was immediate and loud.

'Be serious, man!'

'You're joking, those guys are wimps.'

'They're goody-goods!'

Alex sat up and looked around at his mates; he was embarrassed, but determined to have his say … to make them understand. 'Look at it this way, guys. I'm sick of having nothing to do but biking or skateboarding on the weekends. I'm totally bored, get it? You said, 'There's nothing to do in this place. Well there is. There's Scouts. And if helping others is being a goody-good, I don't mind being one.'

Freedom for What?

Alex continued firmly, 'They aren't wimps, either. Anthony Bryant is in the Scouts and he's no wimp! Just talk to Anthony if you want to know all the cool things they get to do'.

'Yeah, but they go camping and stuff, don't they?' Brendan asked doubtfully. (He'd never been camping before and wasn't sure if he'd like it.)

'Sure they do,' Alex said enthusiastically. 'I love camping out; you get to light fires and cook your dinner. It makes you feel really smart you know, to be able to do that. Doesn't even matter if you burn the sausages a bit when you're camping, you're so hungry that anything tastes OK. Dad used to take Steve and me out camping, but since he got his new job he never has time'.

'You'll have to wear that uniform. You'll look silly,' Cole muttered.

'No I won't, because all the other Scouts will be wearing it, too. Anyway, I reckon the uniform looks smart, and it sure makes you different from everyone else. You've got to admit that!' he finished with a grin.

'You seem to have really thought this out,' Cole said, admiringly.

'I've found out the details and I'm going to go for a few weeks to try it out and see if I'll like it. Anyone want to check it out with me? It'll save you getting bored, and it'll be more fun to go with some friends'. Alex left the question hanging in the air as the others thought about it and mumbled among themselves. (No-one was keen on embarrassing himself in front of the others by saying straight out he'd like to go.)

'Well?' Alex asked, looking at all his friends.

'I might,' Cole said suddenly. 'I'll have to check it out with Mum and Dad first though.'

That did it—now the others had the courage to show they were interested enough to 'check it out' too.

Alex looked at his watch and grabbed his helmet, saying. 'Gotta go, guys, or Mum'll have my "guts for garters"—whatever that means, but she's always saying it! We'll talk some more tomorrow'.

Alex turned to Michael and Brendan, who were on either side him, and grinning he asked, 'So what do you think of Scouts so far?'.

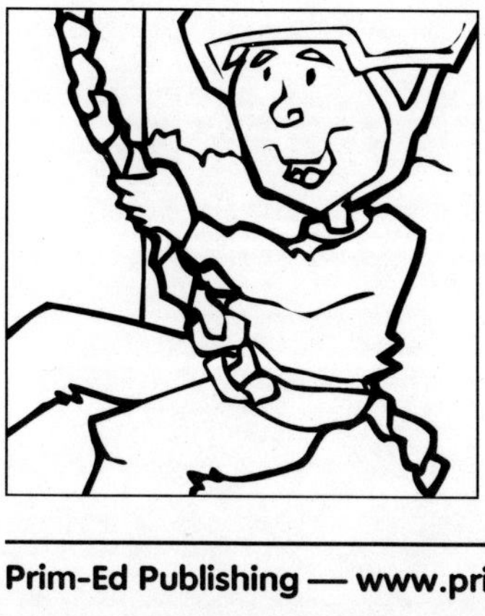

Brendan looked down and gulped and with a sheepish grin replied, 'It's definitely not wimpy!'.

Michael looked over at him and answered, 'I don't mind telling you that this has to be the scariest moment of my life Alex—but I love it!'.

'Yeah, me too, guys, and I'm glad you came to keep me company, too. Now let's finish abseiling off this bridge and see if we can land on the bank next to Cole and the others and not in the river!'.

'Yahoo ... coming down!'

Freedom for What?

A. Tick the circle that gives the best answer for each question.

1. What was 'the gang's' reaction to Alex's idea about joining the Scouts?

○ (a) supportive

● (b) disbelieving

○ (c) angry

○ (d) humorous

○ (e) curious

2. Why did Alex want to join the Scouts?

○ (a) He wanted to go camping.

○ (b) Anthony had asked him to join.

● (c) He wanted more things to do as he was sick of biking and skateboarding.

○ (d) He liked the uniform.

○ (e) He wanted to go abseiling.

3. Just before they sat on the grass talking, the gang had ...

○ (a) been at school.

○ (b) talked about going to Scouts.

○ (c) been abseiling.

● (d) raced their bikes to the top of the hill and back.

○ (e) been skateboarding.

4. What kind of person is a 'wimp'?

○ (a) weak, timid and ineffectual

● (b) easily frightened

○ (c) strong and determined

○ (d) timid and anxious

5. The main idea or point of the story is ...

○ (a) the activities of a gang of boys on the weekend.

○ (b) the benefits of joining Scouts.

● (c) sticking up for something you're keen about against pressure from friends.

○ (d) abseiling is an exciting activity.

Freedom for What?

B. Complete each question as required.

1. True or false?

(a) Anthony Bryant was a wimp.	☐ True	☒ False
(b) All 'the gang' had a drink bottle.	☐ True	☒ False
(c) Alex wanted the other boys to come with him to Scouts.	☒ True	☐ False
(d) Alex was confident about suggesting they all join Scouts.	☒ True	☐ False

2. Cole thought there would be more to 'do' if they lived in the city.

Do you agree? Yes Give a reason for your answer More happening

3. List four activities you can do …

in the city	in the country

4. (a) 'Peer pressure' is often talked about. What is it?

(b) How did Alex resist it?

5. Find the meaning of these words.

(a) determined – Making a decision and not changing it.

(b) occupied – busy or used by Someone.

(c) wistfully – a feeling or regretfull longing

(d) doubtfully – a feeling uncertainty or doubt

The Spooky Story

Alex, Michael, Cole and Brendan were hunched down with their blankets firmly wrapped around their shoulders. The flames of the fire shone an orange glow on their faces and the faces of all the other boys sitting around the fire. Their faces were also reflecting the horror of what they were being told …

'… and the poor man in his long tatty coat was never seen again. No-one found his body, though they looked for months. His dog was found wandering along the road just north of where we are now; it was half starved … and half crazy. Folks around here say that the old man's ghost can be seen wandering around on dark starless nights, holding on to his candle, looking for his dog. He calls the dog by howling for it … Oowooo'.

Although the night was warm, the boys listening shivered and pulled their blankets closer around them. Speculation as to what must have happened to the man now mixed with the fear of seeing his ghost. Furtively, they looked over their shoulders towards the trees.

Michael gripped Brendan's arm and whispered hoarsely, 'Look, no stars tonight'. He gulped his fear down but the lump seemed to stick in his throat.

'Well, lads,' the scoutmaster was standing up to attend to the fire, 'that's it for tonight. Time for bed. Secure your tents because the wind could get up in the night'.

'As long as that's the only thing that gets up in the night!' Paul mumbled.

'Don't worry, Paul,' Michael called. 'It was only a spooky campfire story.'

'Huh, I'm not scared,' Paul denied from the safety of this tent, his torch shining brightly.

'Yeah, sure,' Michael said quietly to Alex with a grin as they headed to their tent.

The site was perfect for a tent camp-out in the 'wilds'. A small stream for water, woods for exploring, and a flat field for pitching tents. The road was on the other side of the woods so any noise from passing traffic was well muffled. The warm night was disturbed only by the noises of the crickets in the woods, the occasional hoot of an owl, and the soft rumbling snores of a couple of sleepers.

Alex woke with a start, and quickly turned his watch alarm off. Cole mumbled and stirred as Alex gently shook Michael and Brendan awake.

'Hey what … is it morning already?' Cole mumbled, trying hard to open his eyes.

'No, you idiot—it's midnight feast time, remember?' Alex replied gently. 'OK guys, get out your goodies, but remember that we'll all have to be really quiet or we'll have to share with anyone we wake up.'

'Huh, let them get their own midnight feast,' Brendan responded.

'Right, Brendan, so what have you got to share? Yum, pineapple chunks. I've got crisps and Michael's brought marshmallows. Did you bring something, Cole?'

'Of course,' he whispered, in a huff. 'Do you think I'd forget that?'

The others all looked at each other and chuckled. It was a well-known fact that Cole was a bit forgetful, but obviously not when his stomach was involved.

The Spooky Story

'Quiet, you idiots,' Cole said, feeling at bit annoyed because the joke had been at his expense. 'We don't want to wake the camp up.'

Passing their loot around, the boys were feeling delightfully naughty, quietly 'pigging out' as they called it. It was innocent fun, although against the rules. The wind started to rise and the tent walls began to flap in and out, gently at first so that they didn't notice, but within 10 minutes the flapping was more demanding and the wind was quite strong.

'Hide those lights, quickly,' Cole whispered suddenly.

'What's up, Cole?' came a whisper from the darkness as the torches went out.

'I think I heard something out there.'

'Just the wind, man,' came a voice.

'Michael,' thought Cole. But the voice didn't sound as confident as Michael's usually did.

'Listen, I can hear something!' Cole hissed savagely.

No-one whispered. No-one even breathed. They were all looking at the tent wall, where a ghostly shadow in a long flapping coat slowly moved past, carrying a candle. The boys' eyeballs looked like they were spring-loaded. They shivered as the hairs on the back of their necks prickled. Their mouths were open and working, but no sound came out.

Finally, Alex croaked in a tiny voice, 'My gosh, it's him!'.

Just as he said that, the figure let out a soft, 'Oowooo'.

Four heads dived under their pillows with one accord and stayed there until morning.

Morning came very slowly for these four scouts and although the sun shone warmly and the birds were singing a dawn chorus, midnight nightmares were remembered. They were the first tent awake, up and dressed. (Having been too scared to sleep soundly since the 'feast', they were already awake when the sun's first rays broke over the camp.) They wandered over to where the scoutmaster was starting the cooking fire. He was limping a bit on his right leg.

'Morning, boys. You're up early. Sleep well?' he asked.

'No, not that good,' Alex finally managed to respond.

'No? Oh, that's all part of the fun of camping, lads. Tents aren't five star hotels you know.'

'What happened to your foot, Sir?' Alex asked, to change the subject.

'Oh, no, you don't want to ask, Alex! In the middle of the night, there I was, all warm and cosy in my tent, the wind tearing about outside like I thought it was going to, and then I realised that I hadn't tied down the trailer cover! I put on my coat, but I couldn't find my torch, so there I was, in the middle of a pitch black night trying to find my way without tripping over the tent pegs! My lighter wasn't much help either, the wind kept blowing it out. I stubbed my toe on one of your tent pegs and oowoo did that hurt. I tried not to wake you up, though. I didn't did I?' His voice sounded puzzled as he had seen a lot of emotion in the four faces. 'It isn't relief, is it? he wondered. 'What are they so relieved about?'

'Well, um, we were already awake actually, Sir, so you didn't wake us,' Michael replied truthfully with his usual confidence, and his cheeky smile appeared once again on his face.

The Spooky Story

A. Tick the circle that gives the best answer for each question.

1. Which two choices tell you how the boys were feeling as they listened to the spooky story?

- ○ (a) … hunched down with their blankets firmly wrapped around their shoulders.
- ○ (b) The flames on the fire shone an orange glow on their faces …
- ○ (c) Furtively, they looked over their shoulders …
- ○ (d) Their faces were also reflecting the horror of what they were being told …

2. Who woke the boys up for the midnight feast?

- ○ (a) Alex
- ○ (b) Cole
- ○ (c) Michael
- ○ (d) Brendan
- ○ (e) The scoutmaster

3. Who was it that the boys heard and saw outside the tent?

- ○ (a) The ghost of the old man.
- ○ (b) Paul going to the toilet.
- ○ (c) The scoutmaster.
- ○ (d) One of the boys from the group scaring them.

4. What did the boys think the 'Oowooo' noise was in the middle of the night?

- ○ (a) The old man's ghost stubbing his toe on the tent peg.
- ○ (b) One of the scouts calling out.
- ○ (c) The scoutmaster stubbing his toe on the tent peg.
- ○ (d) The old man calling for his dog.
- ○ (e) The tent walls flapping in the wind.

5. The boys were relieved because …

- ○ (a) the wind hadn't blown down their tent.
- ○ (b) the scoutmaster hadn't found out about the midnight feast.
- ○ (c) the scoutmaster had already lit the campfire.
- ○ (d) what they had seen outside the tent wasn't the ghost.
- ○ (e) the wind died down during the night.

The Spooky Story

B. Complete each question as required.

1. Give four reasons why the camp site was perfect.

(a) Flat for tents

(b) far from road

(c) woods for exploring

(d) stream of water to drink

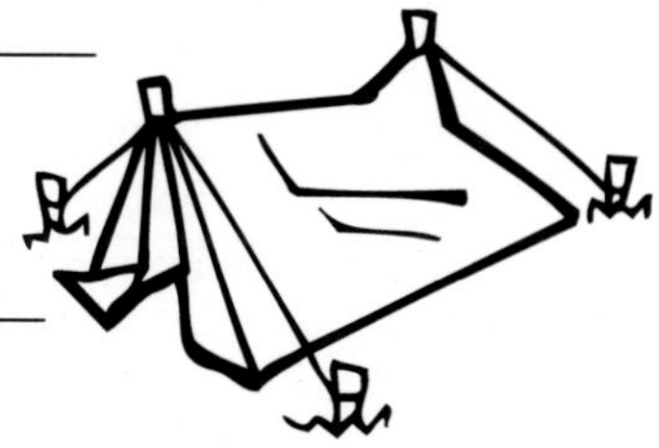

2. True or false?

	True	False
(a) It was a cold night.	☐	☒
(b) Cole had forgotten to bring something for the midnight feast.	☐	☒
(c) Paul was a bit scared.	☒	☐
(d) Alex, Michael, Cole and Brendan were the first tent awake.	☒	☐

3. Find the meanings of these words.

(a) innocent – Not Guilty

(b) secure – Safe

(c) speculation – thinking of a answere without evidence

(d) occasional – Sometimes

4. Complete the following sentences using the words from Question 3.

(a) Rumours that the factory is closing are sheer speculation.

(b) My sister stood by the spilt milk with an innocent look on her face.

(c) I checked that all the windows were secure before I went out.

(d) By stopping for the occasional rest, we made it to the top easily.

5. Explain what is meant by the parts of the sentence in italics.

(a) 'Quiet, you idiots,' Cole said, feeling a bit annoyed *because the joke had been at his expense* …

(b) 'Four heads dived under the pillow *with one accord* …

Heroes Don't Need Medals

It was a hot day. The sun scorched down, and everywhere you looked you could see the heat waves rippling above the sand. Jesse groaned and rolled over, realising that half of his body was well and truly fried! He hadn't meant to doze off in the sun, but the heat and late nights studying for his exams had just crept up on him.

Stretching, he got to his feet, picked up his boogie board, and looked around. The beach, which earlier had been jam-packed with people enjoying the late summer sun, was now comparatively empty. Seagulls swooped down to clean up the remnants of people's picnic lunches. The ice-cream van had vanished, as had the lifesavers.

Jesse looked up to where the sun was and estimated it was about five o'clock. Time to head home. It was 'Mum's Kitchen Rule' that had him moving homewards. If he didn't get home in time for dinner he went hungry. That was the rule and even though Jesse didn't like the restriction this imposed on him, he figured the least he could do was to be home to eat the meal his mum cooked.

His back was beginning to sting and he knew he was going to be sore tomorrow when he had to put his school uniform on again. He groaned at the thought of the teasing his friends were going to give him. Names like 'Hot Stuff' and 'Lobster' would be the order of the day. 'Sometimes friends can be so predictable,' he thought.

Wandering along the water's edge, kicking at the foam, he happened to glance out to sea. What made him look at this particular moment he never knew, but it was the right time for the swimmer he spotted, who was obviously in trouble. His hand was up in the accepted distress signal, and he was calling out something. Quickly, Jesse glanced around the beach—no-one else was close enough to help the man.

Cupping his hands to his mouth he shouted, 'Help' to get the attention of other people on the beach. Someone waved back to him and Jesse pointed to the swimmer, 'Get help,' he shouted. Then without hesitation he plunged into the surf with his boogie board trailing behind him.

Jesse wasn't being stupid ... or even consciously brave. Heroes seem to act first without conscious thought, to aid a fellow human. Thinking about danger comes later when they freely admit that if they'd stopped to think of the risks involved, they wouldn't have done the deed. However, Jesse was in fact a very strong swimmer. He had started swimming at the age of eight so he could earn his swimming badge at Cubs, and he'd just never stopped swimming. He had good stamina for distance swimming and his coach had tried hard to persuade him to go into competitions, but he wasn't interested in all that. He swam for enjoyment, not for medals. And now today he was swimming for more than enjoyment or medals ... he was swimming to save someone's life.

His strokes were strong as he cut through the water. 'I must be close to him now,' he thought. Then he heard the man cry, 'Help me, I've got cramp, please help'.

The man was only metres away, but was floundering badly and looked to be panicking. As soon as Jesse reached him, he started to reassure him, 'It's OK, mister, you'll be OK. I'll get you to shore'.

Heroes Don't Need Medals

'Easier said than done.' Jesse thought silently. 'This guy is a big fella.' Speaking calmly, he helped the man get on his board. The guy was exhausted and weak but he understood what Jesse was saying. He clung on to the front of the boogie board but that was all he seemed capable of doing.

'His leg must still be cramped. Lucky the sea isn't rough and there's no rip,' Jesse thought as he started swimming back to shore, towing the board behind him.

As he reached the shallow water, willing hands appeared to help carry the man ashore. He sat down and began to recover his breath. A small crowd had gathered around the swimmer. He seemed to be getting the attention he needed. Someone was putting him in the recovery position and someone else was running up to the cars for blankets.

'They must know what they're doing,' Jesse thought, reaching for his board and standing up. Feeling tired but better than he'd felt in his life before, he figured that since no-one needed him he'd better get home before he missed out on his dinner.

No-one noticed him leave.

A. Tick the circle that gives the best answer for each question.

1. Jesse was …

- ○ (a) at the beach with a group of his friends.
- ◉ (b) at the beach by himself.
- ○ (c) with a group of friends early in the afternoon but they went home.
- ○ (d) meant to meet some friends at the beach but they didn't turn up.

2. Choose the words you think best describe Jesse.

- ○ (a) thoughtful, panicky, brave
- ○ (b) selfish, level-headed, brave
- ◉ (c) thoughtful, level-headed, brave
- ○ (d) pleasant, level-headed, uncertain

3. Why did Jesse choose not to swim competitively?

- ◉ (a) He wasn't interested.
- ◉ (b) He didn't swim to win medals.
- ○ (c) He didn't enjoy swimming.
- ○ (d) He wasn't fit enough.

4. What were the conditions at the beach like?

- ○ (a) It was windy.
- ○ (b) The sea was rough.
- ○ (c) There was a strong rip.
- ◉ (d) It was calm and sunny.

Heroes Don't Need Medals

B. Complete each question as required.

1. Order the sentences.

[2] (a) Jesse helped the man onto the board.

[4] (b) Jesse swam back to the shore, towing the board.

[3] (c) The man clung onto the board.

[1] (d) Jesse reassured the man.

2. Jesse's Mum had a rule that he had to be home for dinner at a certain time. Jesse felt that this was a restriction imposed on him. While he didn't like it, he did adhere to it because he felt it was only fair to his Mum.
Think of a restriction that is imposed on you at home and at school. Say how you feel about each and why.

Home ______________________________

____

____

School ______________________________

____

____

3. Find the meaning of these words.

(a) comparatively – compared to somthing else

(b) estimated – A rough guess

(c) predictable – Knowing whats going to happen

(d) stamina – The amount that you can be attive at a time

(e) imposed – A decision

4. Complete the following sentences using the words from Question 3.

(a) It takes a great deal of stamina to complete a marathon.

(b) The response of the crowd to the player being sent off was Pradictable as they had always been a vocal crowd.

(c) The builder estimated the repair job would take him a week.

(d) The clothes I bought in Hong Kong were comparativey cheap to those here.

(e) The council imposed a fine for dumping rubbish.

The Bike Tube

'If I've heard it before, I've heard it a hundred times,' thought Brett glumly. 'Sorry, Brett, but we can't afford it.'

It was a standard answer any time he needed money for something. Brett knew it was difficult for his parents. They worked hard in their business but they'd had some bad luck with people not paying them, and it had really set them back. He understood that they had to be careful about what they spent, and luxuries like movies and bought lunches were definitely out. But Brett hadn't thought that a new inner tube for his bike was a luxury, because he needed it to ride to school every day. Now he was going to have to get up earlier in the mornings, because he'd have to walk to school … and that was five kilometres! 'At least,' he thought to himself, 'I'm going to get fit for the football tournament'.

Brett wandered outside, his hands jammed in his pockets, kicking at the stones on the unsealed driveway. The dust covered his shoes. He was sick of this 'can't afford it' business. His mother said, 'We're not poor Brett, we're only temporarily broke, and our family is lucky to be rich with love. That's better than having a load of money and being miserable'.

Brett privately thought that 'temporarily' seemed like 'forever'. He also thought that if he had a load of money he was darn sure that it would make him happy. He did realise though that his parents were right, too, because he'd seen that some of his 'rich' friends were not happy at home. Their parents were always working and they were left to their own devices most of the time. He was lucky that his mum was there to help with his homework or just to listen to him if he had a good (or bad) day.

Sitting down on the grass, Brett decided that he really needed to get his bike fixed, and if he couldn't get the money from his parents, he'd better do something about it himself.

'If it is to be, it's up to me,' he quoted to himself with a grin. Having made that decision he started to think of ways to earn the money. Lawnmowing was probably out, because people who didn't do it themselves usually got the 'lawnmower man' to do it every week—but it could be worth a try.

Picking a daisy, he absently picked the petals off one by one, while his brain worked overtime on his major problem. What do people in my neighbourhood need? Let's start with basics—everyone needs food, warmth and shelter.

Well, for food I could fetch groceries for older folks … there's old Mrs Barry down the street—she has bad legs and might want that help. And there's a load of vegetables in our veggie patch and apples on the tree. I'll ask Mum if I can sell some! Brett was getting excited now, he could see real possibilities … solutions to his problem, and it was going to be fun, too!

'Now, warmth is next,' he thought. It was autumn now and he'd noticed loads of firewood in some of his neighbours' driveways. Perhaps he could stack the wood for them. If he told them why he wanted to work, they might even find other jobs for him to do. He could babysit. He was good with little kids … in fact, they were a lot of fun to play with.

The Bike Tube

Running into the kitchen he yelled, 'Mum, Mum, where's some paper?'. Finding some on the bench, he grabbed a pen and started to write all his moneymaking ideas down. As his mother came and leant over his shoulder to see what he was so excited about, he asked, 'Mum, is it OK with you and Dad if I go around the neighbourhood earning some money?'.

'No problem, Brett, in fact I'm proud of you for thinking of it. One thing, though … you must not just ask for money, you have to earn it. If someone thinks you've done a good job and pays you a bit extra, well that's fine. Remember to be polite and well-mannered won't you?'

'Yeah, sure Mum, of course I will,' Brett said as he took off out the door. 'I'm going to visit Mrs O'Donnell first to see if she wants that firewood stacked up'.

Three hours later the front door burst wide open as Brett came racing inside.

'Yippee. Yes, yes, yes! Look, Mum, I've earnt £13 already on my first day, and Mr Kennedy said I could wash his car on the weekend, too … cars always need washing, don't they? He might want me back if I do a good job, do you think? By the way, Dad, how much is a bike tube?'

A. Tick the circle that gives the best answer for each question.

1. Brett wanted the money …

- ○ (a) to buy lunch at school.
- ○ (b) to go to the movies.
- ○ (c) to buy a new inner tube.
- ○ (d) to buy a new bike.

2. Brett's family didn't have much money because …

- ○ (a) his dad had been made redundant.
- ○ (b) his mum didn't work.
- ○ (c) they'd had bad luck in their business.
- ○ (d) they were careless with money.

3. How did Brett feel about the money situation?

- ○ (a) He understood but he couldn't help feeling frustrated about it.
- ○ (b) He thought it was unreasonable and argued with his parents.
- ○ (c) He felt frustrated and was really upset with his parents.
- ○ (d) He understood and didn't mind at all.

4. By coming up with the money making scheme, Brett showed …

- ○ (a) dependence.
- ○ (b) perseverance.
- ○ (c) disobedience.
- ○ (d) initiative.

The Bike Tube

B. Complete each question as required.

1. What do you think may have happened after Brett's initial success at Mrs O'Donnell's? Give two different possibilities.

(a) ____________________

(b) ____________________

2. Complete the sentences.

(a) 'Walking to school will make me fit for the football tournament,' thought Brett.

(b) Brett knew that many of his friends were left to their own devices most of the time after school because their parents worked.

(c) Brett decided to do jobs around his neighbourhood.

3. Explain a way you currently do earn money, or detail a way you could earn money if you found yourself in a situation like Brett's.

____

____

____

____

____

4. Find the meaning of these words or phrases.

(a) luxuries – An inessential desirable item.

(b) temporarily – Not forever.

(c) own devices – To allow someone to do what they want.

(d) absently – distrated or gone.

5. Complete the sentences using the words from Question 4.

(a) When he was left to his own devices, the young boy didn't cope very well.

(b) Kim absenty scribbled on her pad as she listened to the teacher.

(c) After winning the cash prize, the old lady was able to afford some of the luxuries she had to go without.

(d) Because of a major flood, the road north was temporarily closed.

No-one Special

It was morning and Kelly looked at herself in the mirror in disgust. She had prayed hard last night to God to make her beautiful, but she still looked the same. The same ugly freckles, the same snub nose (that Mum thought was cute), and wild, curly red hair that she could never seem to get looking tidy.

Why wasn't God listening? She had prayed hard every night for the last three weeks and she was starting to feel that it was hopeless.

As she got ready for school she hummed a little tune; well, you have to keep yourself positive somehow! After putting on her coat and cycle helmet she grabbed her bike. She'd just make it to class on time if she hurried.

She was only round the corner from school when it happened!

A young child running to school slipped over in a puddle and went sprawling onto the footpath. The child's bag flew open and her lunch rolled into the puddle. There was no-one else around and Kelly had almost passed her when it happened. Well it was none of her business anyway, was it, and Mr Andrews had said if she was late again this week he'd put her on detention. She couldn't do detention, she had to do her paper round after school and then her homework.

The little girl was crying loudly and holding her leg. Kelly couldn't bear it any longer. No way was she leaving a little kid hurt like that without stopping and trying to help.

Propping her bike against the fence, Kelly bent down and spoke kindly.

'Hi, my name's Kelly, where are you hurt?' she asked the child gently.

The child sobbed quietly as Kelly looked at her badly cut knee. 'At least it's a clean wound,' Kelly thought to herself as she carefully tied her large clean hanky around it. 'Not terrific but it'll do. Good thing we're close to school!'

'Would you like to tell me your name?'

'Jamie,' the child whispered between sobs. 'My name's Jamie.'

'Well, Jamie, let's see if you can stand on that leg now. That's it, good girl. Can you sit on my bike if I lift you up on it?'

Kelly picked up Jamie's bag and lunch. 'The lunch isn't any good now,' she thought, looking at the soggy sandwiches. Together they managed to get Jamie up on the bike and Kelly carefully began walking to school.

Once at school she piggybacked Jamie to the office.

As the school secretary examined Jamie's knee, Kelly filled out the accident form and signed it with her name and class number.

'I'd better scram' she said out loud, and grabbing her bag headed for the door. Suddenly she stopped, 'Oh, here, Mrs Carter, give Jamie my lunch, will you please,' she said as she dug it out of her bag. 'Hers fell in a puddle.' And off she ran to class.

No-one Special

'Just my luck, I'm in for it now,' Kelly muttered to herself as she saw her teacher glaring at her. The day had started badly for Kelly and it seemed to go from bad to worse! She'd been growled at in front of the whole class for being late and wasn't allowed to say why she was late. Then there was the maths test! Maths, Kelly decided, just wasn't her best subject. At break the kids teased her for being on detention and then lunchtime came and she had no lunch, of course. To top it all off she'd have to finish her paper round in the dark.

Kelly moaned, sometimes it was so hard to stay happy. The last of her papers had been delivered. Pushing her bike up the hill towards her house she was just too tired, cold and hungry to hum a happy tune. She still had her homework to do.

As she came in the door, Dad said, 'Kelly, you had a visitor while you were out, a Mrs Johnson. She left this for you.'

Kelly raised her head and stared at her father in surprise. 'Who's Mrs Johnson? I don't know any Johnsons.'

'Well, this letter and parcel have your name on them, so she must know you,' her Dad said. 'What does it say?'

Kelly opened the envelope and took out the letter. She read it in the silence, her eyes widening in surprise and pleasure.

'Well?' demanded Dad from the doorway. 'What is it all about?'

'It's a letter of thanks, Dad. I helped a little girl this morning, that's why I was late to school and got a detention. This is a letter from her mum to say "Thanks". It's a really nice letter.'

'Wow!' exclaimed Dad as he finished the letter. 'And they put you on detention for helping a little kid?'

'The teacher didn't let me explain why I was late, Dad,' Kelly said absently, as she unwrapped the small parcel. Inside the wrapping was the hanky that she'd used to bandage Jamie's knee, all clean and ironed. Under her hanky was a little, old-looking, black velvet box. Carefully, Kelly opened the box. Inside lay a gold chain with a heart-shaped locket. Engraved on it was the inscription, 'I am special'.

Kelly stared at it with tears in her eyes. She didn't even hear Dad say that he was going to inform her teacher just what made her late, and demand an apology for not allowing her to give her reasons.

The next morning, when once again Kelly looked at herself in the mirror, she smiled. Her whole face lit up and she looked beautiful. She smiled at herself ... then it must be true what they say; true beauty comes from within you, and when you let your heart guide you in your actions, others can see your beauty too! 'Isn't it amazing,' she thought, 'what feeling good about yourself can do!'.

She lightly fingered the little golden locket around her neck. In future she decided, whenever I feel 'ugly' I'll just touch this locket and remember its message ... I am special'.

No-one Special

A. Tick the circle that gives the best answer for each question.

1. Which word best describes how Kelly felt about the way she looked?

○ (a) content

○ (b) dissatisfied

○ (c) ecstatic

○ (d) complacent

○ (e) positive

2. Why did Kelly hesitate before she stopped to help Jamie?

○ (a) She didn't like small children.

○ (b) She was worried about being put on detention.

○ (c) She hated the sight of blood.

○ (d) She thought it was none of her business.

○ (e) both (b) and (d).

3. How far was Kelly from school when the accident happened?

○ (a) around the corner

○ (b) several streets away

○ (c) several kilometres away

○ (d) a street away

○ (e) near her home

4. Why was Kelly put on detention?

○ (a) She didn't do her homework.

○ (b) She was late for school.

○ (c) She failed a Maths test.

○ (d) She didn't like Maths.

5. Choose the sentence which you think best explains what the main idea of the story is.

○ (a) It is good to help others.

○ (b) If you help others you get presents.

○ (c) What you do and how others react make a difference to how you feel about yourself.

○ (d) You feel good when you help others.

No-one Special

B. Complete each question as required.

1. What things made Kelly's day go from bad to worse?

____

____

____

2. Order the sentences.

[3] (a) Kelly gave her lunch to Jamie.
[1] (b) The little girl slipped and fell.
[4] (c) Mr Andrews gave Kelly detention.
[5] (d) Kelly came home from her paper round.
[2] (e) Kelly took Jamie to school on her bike.
[6] (f) Mrs Johnson left a present for Kelly.

3. (i) For each word in bold print, colour whether it is a noun, adjective or a verb in the sentence given. Write the meaning of each word.

(ii) Each of the highlighted words can also be used as a different 'part of speech'. When used in this way it has a slightly different meaning. Write the meaning of each word.

(a) 'The same ugly freckles, the same **snub** nose ...'

(i) *Noun* | *Verb* | *Adjective*

meaning ignore or rebuffs

(ii) meaning Movement

(b) 'Kelly couldn't **bear** it any longer ...'

(i) *Noun* | *Verb* | *Adjective*

meaning couldn't handle it

(ii) meaning Animal

(c) 'Can you sit on my bike if I can **lift** you up on it?'

(i) *Noun* | *Verb* | *Adjective*

meaning To pick Something up

(ii) meaning Elevator

Night Fright

Carl was eleven years old now and he thought that he was fairly grown up. After all, he was in his seventh year at school. It seemed to Carl that life was pretty unfair. His parents (and teachers) were often telling him things like 'It's your responsibility' and 'You are old enough to know better', yet they weren't very willing, it seemed, to treat him like an adult.

Take tomorrow night, for example. Tomorrow was Saturday and Carl's mum and dad were going to an adult movie. They could have let him see one of the more suitable 'family' movies on at the same time, but no, he had to say home. Not only did he have to stay home, he had to have a babysitter!

'But, Mum, I'm eleven years old, I don't need a babysitter!' he wailed (sounding more like five years old than eleven).

'Sorry, Carl, but even though we know we can trust you at home by yourself, I feel happier knowing you have someone older with you. Besides, you know that the police don't recommend leaving children under fourteen years old at home unsupervised,' his mother replied. Carl did know, but he wasn't at all happy with the idea, and he walked away grumbling under his breath.

It was Saturday night already and the babysitter, Mrs Bennett, was being welcomed at the front door. She was a friend of his mother and lived over by Carl's school not far away. Carl looked at the TV guide then tossed it down in disgust. Nothing interesting on TV tonight, he may as well go up to his bedroom and read his book. It was one of those adventure books where you can choose your own ending and determine the plot, depending on what decisions you make as you go along.

Carl had read it once already and he was looking forward to reading it again and making the hero act differently from the last time. It would be a whole new plot and ending. These books (as far as Carl was concerned) were more fun than playing computer games and much better than ordinary storybooks where the story and endings have already been decided on by the author. Magic, monsters and mayhem, and a human hero … you! Fantasy at its best!

He had curled up on his bed with the book, The Quest of the Golden Crystal, and was relaxed and deeply involved in the story when, suddenly, there was a loud banging and clanging on the roof above him. He looked up, startled, and wondered if it was another cat on the roof from the nearby trees. He was about to return to his reading when all of a sudden there was a most terrifying loud screech!

Carl nearly leapt out of his skin in fright, and lay on the bed hardly daring to breathe. More loud banging on the roof made him suddenly decide he might be more comfortable in the lounge (where Mrs Bennett was). Making a grab for his book, he took off into the lounge, not even bothering to turn off the light.

Mrs Bennett looked up as he entered the room. She was watching a noisy movie on television. It looked like one of those old (but scary) horror movies. Turning the volume down she asked, 'Is something the matter Carl? You look a bit pale'.

'Didn't you hear that horrible noise, that screeching noise?' Carl queried.

Night Fright

'Noise, Carl, what noise? I didn't hear anything. Mind you. I do have the TV up quite loud I guess. I'm sure it was nothing to worry about.'

Carl was still quite shaken and he hadn't figured out what could have made the noise. The goosebumps were raised on his arms as he tried to explain to Mrs Bennett what the noise sounded like. Mrs Bennett could see that Carl was upset, but she didn't really believe that he had heard a noise that sounded like those pterodactyl dinosaur 'birds' that he'd seen on videos. She was just telling Carl that the noise must have been a cat when the next horrendous screech split the air.

'Great heavens!' Mrs Bennett screamed (almost as loud as Carl) as she jumped in fright. Her eyes were the size of dinner plates and she had lost some of her colour. Visions of the horror movie started wafting through her mind, just a mental picture of the ogres and monsters from his book had taken a determined hold on Carl's unwilling imagination. They stared at each other for a minute as they tried to collect their scattered thoughts. Mrs Bennett was the first to move.

Taking the torch from the top of the fridge, she said in what she hoped was a firm voice (but in reality wasn't much more than a whisper), 'I'll take a look out back'.

However, as she approached the back door another episode of banging, accompanied by another couple of short screeches, put a damper on that idea and she decided to stay right where she was, inside. Anyway, she certainly wasn't getting paid for this ... only to babysit!

Just as quietly, she said to Carl, 'Whatever it is, it's staying out there'. (And to herself she added 'And I'm staying in here!'.) Having made that decision, she decided that a warm drink of hot chocolate would help them more than a torch.

They heard no more noises of any kind after that, so Carl figured that the 'monster' had given up on trying to entice them out of the house to eat them, and had taken off to try somewhere else. He wasn't able to read any more of his book for the night. Mrs Bennett didn't want to continue watching the horror movie either, so they ended up playing cards until Carl went to bed and fell into a troubled sleep.

Carl was still a bit groggy with sleep as he staggered out for breakfast the next morning. The smell of bacon and eggs hung in the air and the sounds of his mother busily moving about in the kitchen helped him to clear his head a little. Then he remembered last night. Seeing his father, be began to tell him about it. 'Dad ...' was a far as he got.

His father rushed passed him, a frown on his face. 'Sorry Carl, ... can't stop, I'm late for work this morning. Those darn owls kept me awake last night. Gotta go ... Bye'. He slammed the door behind him.

Carl's mother caught the look of confusion on Carl's face and explained, 'The young owls are learning to fly, unfortunately for us, so at various intervals during the night, we were awakened by the thumps and screeching as the babies fell on the roof and I guess were picked up by their parents. What a racket it made—it's a good thing you slept through it'.

Absorbing that information, Carl came to the conclusion that even though he was almost 'grown up', he was still pleased that he'd had a 'babysitter' with him last night!

Night Fright

A. Tick the circle that gives the best answer for each question.

1. How did Carl feel about having a babysitter?

○ (a) pleased

○ (b) didn't care

○ (c) unhappy

○ (d) very annoyed

2. What was Carl doing when he heard the first screech?

○ (a) playing a computer

○ (b) reading a book

○ (c) watching the movie with Mrs Bennett

○ (d) finishing homework

○ (e) playing cards

3. How did Mrs Bennett know he was upset?

○ (a) He told her.

○ (b) He was crying.

○ (c) He looked a bit pale.

○ (d) She'd heard the screech, too.

○ (e) He looked worried.

4. Why do you think Mrs Bennett didn't finish watching the horror movie?

○ (a) She wasn't enjoying it and couldn't be bothered finishing it.

○ (b) She was too busy trying to find the cause of the noises.

○ (c) Carl's mum and dad came home from the movies.

○ (d) The noises had unnerved her and she was feeling nervous enough.

5. What was the cause of the noise?

○ (a) baby owls screeching to be fed

○ (b) baby owls learning to fly

○ (c) baby owls being chased by a cat

○ (d) both (a) and (b)

○ (e) both (b) and (c)

Night Fright

B. Complete each question as required.

1. The baby owls were learning to fly at night because owls are nocturnal. Give a definition of nocturnal and then research another animal which is nocturnal. Write two interesting facts about that animal.

Nocturnal means ______

1. sleep during the day

2. awake at night

2. Sequence these events.

- [7] (a) Dad went to work in a hurry because he was late.
- [2] (b) Mrs Bennett, the babysitter, arrived.
- [4] (c) Carl went into the lounge because he heard a loud noise.
- [1] (d) Carl was feeling 'put out' because he had to have a babysitter.
- [6] (e) Mrs Bennett decided against investigating the noise.
- [8] (f) Mum explained about the noises which had kept her and Dad awake in the night.
- [5] (g) Mrs Bennett heard the noise too.
- [3] (h) Carl read in his room.

3. Carl enjoyed 'pick a path' books where he could decide on the story as he went and choose his own ending. What type of books do you enjoy reading? Why?

______

______

4. Find the meaning of these words.

(a) responsibility – in control

(b) unsupervised – on your own

(c) absorbed – Take something in

(d) determine – Figure out

5. Complete the sentences using the words from Question 4.

(a) The children were left unsupervised at the pool, which caused pool staff some concern.

(b) It is our responsibility to determine whether the proposed new factory will damage the environment.

(c) As Mum absorbed the news of my sister's accident from the police officer, her face creased with concern.

The Date

Leanne opened her eyes and looked at the clock. The luminous dial glowed red in the bedroom. 'Two-fifteen,' she groaned to herself. 'It feels like it should be morning by now. I can't see myself suddenly nodding off now when I've been trying to get to sleep for the last five hours. It's going to be a long night, that's for sure.'

As she lay in bed, her mind automatically played a review of the last three days. Why couldn't she clear her head? It kept going around and around like a broken record. Whose fault was it anyway? It wasn't hers. Not really.

It had all started when Paul asked her to the movies on Saturday. She'd been really pleased. Paul was a very cool guy. He'd never paid her much attention before, probably because he was too busy noticing Rachel Johns, the prettiest girl in the class. She never thought to ask Paul why he'd asked her out and not Rachel. Who cared? She didn't! … until now … and now could be too late!

So she'd gone to the movies with Paul. She was fifteen years old, and her mother said it was OK as long as she was home by eleven. The movies had finished around ten so they'd grabbed a drink and chips to eat on the way home. Paul had been very polite. He'd walked her up to her door and said goodnight to her (and to her parents who where hovering in the hallway). And he'd thanked her for going out with him.

And that was it! Well, it was no big deal, just another date with another boy. She knew she wasn't exactly ugly because she'd been on dates a few other times, although she preferred to go with a group of friends rather than with one boy. However, Paul had been fun to go out with and she'd really enjoyed herself. She hoped he might ask her again, but he hadn't as yet.

So it came as quite a shock to Leanne to find the note in her desk on Monday. Opening it quickly she stared at the words written in felt pen.

'*See Paul again and you'll be sorry.*'

She glanced around to see if anybody was looking at her. No-one seemed to be. She screwed it up and got out her books.

At lunchtime she saw Paul coming over to join her under the shade of the tree to eat lunch. Should she mention the note in her desk, she wondered? No, it seemed such a silly thing now.

'Good movie last Saturday, Paul. Thanks for taking me to see it.'

'That's OK, Leanne. I wanted to see it myself, and it's more fun to go with someone than to go alone, isn't it?' Paul replied.

'You're not wrong there, Paul. I hate going by myself.'

'Well, maybe we'll do it another time?'

'Sure thing, Paul. I'd like that,' Leanne answered. The conversation was the sort you'd have with a friend. Nothing personal, no promises, nothing special.

The Date

However, someone must have heard or seen them talking and put a different meaning to it, because more anonymous notes began appearing in Leanne's school desk. And these weren't silly, they were full of threats … and hate.

'*If you ever speak to Paul again I'll get you, and your face will be so ugly no-one will want to speak to you. I'll be watching.*'

That was the worst one. It scared her so much she kept looking around at school to see who was watching her. She also avoided getting near or talking to Paul.

Leanne was hot. Her electric blanket must be still on. Rolling over she reached down and turned it off. Settling back down, her mind again went back to her problem. The hate mail … the threats … who on earth could it be? She couldn't think that any of the boys she'd dated would be so jealous of her going out with another guy that they'd do this.

And what was she going to do about it?

She'd have to do something … and soon. She was getting to be a nervous wreck. She jumped when anyone talked to her and she couldn't concentrate on her lessons because of worrying. And the worrying was giving her nightmares … when she did finally manage to sleep! The only thing she could think to do was talk to Paul about it. Maybe he could help her somehow. As she came to this decision the worry seemed to lift from her mind, allowing her to relax. Slowly, she drifted into a deep, dreamless, sleep—the best sleep for three nights. She was feeling better in the morning and by lunchtime had a plan of how to talk to Paul, hopefully without being seen.

Twenty past three. Paul should be home. Leanne picked up the telephone and dialled his number.

'Paul? Hi, it's Leanne here. Listen, I need to talk to you. It's really important but I can't meet you anywhere public. I know it sounds silly, but could you come to my place?'

'Well, OK, Leanne, if it's important. What's it all about?'

'I can't tell you over the phone, Paul. Could you come through the park which backs on to our back garden? I'll open our gate. Don't come up the street. OK?'

'OK. I'll come over now. You've got me really curious. See you soon.'

Leanne waited at the bottom of her garden and saw Paul coming through the park. She looked carefully all around. Good, there didn't seem to be anybody watching Paul or following him.

'Well, Leanne here I am. Now, what's the big mystery?' asked Paul as she closed the gate.

'Take a look at these, Paul. Someone put them in my desk.' She handed the notes to him, even the first one that she'd screwed up. She'd saved them all.

'What on earth? Who sent them?' he exclaimed.

'I don't know. That's why I've been avoiding you, Paul, I'm scared. I can't sleep without having nightmares about it.'

Paul sat silently on he grass, deep in thought. Leanne said nothing. Finally, he looked up.

'I've got it. We'll have to set a trap for them.'

The Date

'Well, OK. But how?'

'Hmm, let's see now … this person always leaves the notes in your desk, right? Not your bag or locker?'

'Yes. Always in my desk. First thing in the morning and lunchtimes.'

'Well, let's see if we can catch them putting the notes in.'

'But I haven't had any since I stopped talking to you.'

'Then we'd better make sure we bait the trap by having lunch together tomorrow. If it works, the next letter will be put in your desk first thing Friday morning. This is a serious case of bullying you know. Bullying isn't just physical, it can take other forms as well, such as picking on someone all the time or calling them names. Our teacher will have to be told. You'd better let me take the notes to show him. He may be able to recognise the writing.'

'Thanks a lot, Paul. That's a load off my mind. Sorry to get you into this mess though.'

'Hey, what are friends for? See you at lunch tomorrow, Leanne.'

Leanne parked her bicycle and walked towards her classroom. It was Friday morning. She was still scared … scared they'd caught the person responsible for the hate mail … and scared they hadn't!

She'd had lunch with Paul yesterday as planned, and they chatted together at morning break, too.

They kept their eyes open, trying to see if anyone was paying any particular attention to them, but they didn't notice anyone.

As she hung up her bag she heard a commotion coming from the classroom. Going in she saw Paul near her desk with the teacher. Rachel was screaming, 'It's Leanne's fault. It's all her fault. If she hadn't gone out with Paul we'd still be together. She broke us up … I'll scratch her eyes out when I see her again'.

'Rachel,' said Paul quietly, 'it was over between you and me well before I took Leanne to the movies. It's not her fault. You just couldn't accept that. I'm sorry, but you can't go around threatening people and making their lives a misery like that'.

'Come along, young lady,' Mr Winters said sternly. 'I think we'd best go and see the head teacher about this. Good morning, Leanne. You and Paul may be required to come over later. I'll let you know.'

'Yes, Mr Winters.'

'Leanne,' Paul moved closer, concern showing on his face, 'are you all right? Here sit down; you look a bit pale'.

'I'm OK, Paul. Was it really Rachel? But why?'

'You heard her, she was jealous. Sometimes people feel so jealous and resentful it can eat away at them until they can't think straight. I hope Rachel is given some counselling to help her learn to cope with her feelings. She's not a bad person; just mixed up at the moment.'

'Well I'm glad that it's all out in the open now. I was making myself ill by worrying.'

The Date

A. Tick the circle that gives the best answer for each question.

1. Leanne couldn't sleep because …

○ (a) she had been on a date with Paul and couldn't stop thinking about it.

○ (b) she was going on her date with Paul and couldn't stop thinking about it.

○ (c) she was worried about the threatening notes she had received in her desk.

○ (d) she was worried that Paul would get too serious.

○ (e) she was worried about an exam.

2. Select the best group of words to describe Paul.

○ (a) thoughtful, level-headed, good fun

○ (b) macho, level-headed, good fun

○ (c) boastful, thoughtless, calm, kind

○ (d) good sportsman, calm, kind

3. After the movies, Leanne and Paul …

○ (a) got a drink, some chips and walked home.

○ (b) got a drink and some chips before Leanne's dad picked them up.

○ (c) walked straight home.

○ (d) got a drink and walked home.

○ (e) got some chips and walked home.

4. Why did Rachel put the notes in Leanne's desk?

○ (a) If Rachel couldn't go out with Paul she didn't want anyone else to, either.

○ (b) Rachel didn't like Leanne.

○ (c) Rachel really wanted to go out with Paul.

○ (d) Rachel and Paul had broken up and she blamed Leanne.

5. Leanne heard a 'commotion' in the classroom. What word best describes a 'commotion'?

○ (a) noise

○ (b) disturbance

○ (c) screaming

○ (d) explosion

○ (e) riot

The Date

B. Complete each question as required.

1. Tick all the things that had to be done to 'set the trap'.

- [ ] (a) Leanne had to tell her mum and dad.
- [x] (b) Leanne and Paul had to be seen together.
- [x] (c) Paul had to speak to the teacher.
- [x] (d) The teacher had to speak to the head teacher.
- [ ] (e) Leanne and Paul had to stay away from each other.

2. What do you think the main message of the author is?

____

____

3. Comment on the ways Leanne went about solving her problem.
Say whether you think they would be appropriate and realistic in a real-life situation.

____

____

____

4. Is bullying an issue at your school? Comment on why or why not.

____

____

____

5. Write the meaning of each word and write a sentence on the back of this sheet which shows this meaning clearly.

(a) luminous – bright light

(b) automatically – happen on its own.

(c) anonymous – unknown

(d) avoiding – Purposely not doing something

Answers

Pages 1–3 Fried Eggs

A. 1. (a) 2. (d) 3. (c) 4. (a)

B. 1. (e) (a) (c) (b) (d)
2. (a) fishing (b) plastic
(c) skating (d) fried
3. Because she'd done things that she wanted to do and forgotten her father's birthday.
4. (a) subconscious – the part of your mind below consciousness or awareness
(b) clue – something which helps to explain a puzzle or a mystery
(c) anatomy – the structure of an animal or plant
(d) detract – to reduce the value of
5. Teacher check

Pages 4–6 Daydreamer

A. 1. (c) 2. (a) 3. (b) 4. (b) 5. (d)

B. 1. (a) true (b) false (c) true (d) true (e) false
2. The drawing should be like the description in the story.
3. Teacher check
4. Teacher check
5. Teacher check. Examples: actress, band member, graphic designer, set designer, busker, author etc.

Pages 7–10 Freedom for What?

A. 1. (b) 2. (c) 3. (d) 4. (a) 5. (c)

B. (a) false (b) false (c) true (d) false
2. Teacher check
3. Teacher check
4. (a) when your friends talk you into doing something you don't want to do; or out of something you do want to do
(b) Teacher check
5. (a) determined – firm in purpose
(b) occupied – involved in, busy
(c) wistfully – thoughtful in a sad way
(d) doubtfully – a feeling of uncertainty

Pages 11–14 The Spooky Story

A. 1. (c) and (d) 2. (a) 3. (c) 4. (d)
5. (d) although (b) could be justified.

B. 1. (a) A small stream for water
(b) Woods for exploring
(c) A flat field for pitching the tents
(d) The road was on the other side of the woods so the traffic noise was muffled.
2. (a) false (b) false (c) true (d) true
3. (a) innocent – free from guilt or from having done anything wrong
(b) secure – firmly fastened or in place
(c) speculation – to think over or have an opinion without certain knowledge
(d) occasional – happening sometimes
4. (a) speculation (b) innocent (c) secure
(d) occasional
5. (a) He was annoyed because the joke had been about him.
(b) Four heads dived under the pillow at the same time.

Pages 15–17 Heroes Don't Need Medals

A. 1. (b) 2. (c) 3. (a) 4. (d)

B. 1. (d) (a) (c) (b)
2. Teacher check
3. (a) comparatively – thought about by comparison, to something else relatively
(b) estimated – roughly guessed
(c) predictable – to tell what will happen in the future
(d) stamina – physical strength or power, especially to fight off tiredness
(e) imposed – to set something to be obeyed
4. (a) stamina (b) predictable
(c) estimated (d) comparatively
(e) imposed

Pages 18–20 The Bike Tube

A. 1. (c) 2. (c) 3. (a) 4. (d)

B. 1. Teacher check
2. (a) football (b) devices
(c) neighbourhood
3. Teacher check
4. (a) luxuries – anything that makes life extremely pleasant or comfortable
(b) temporarily – lasting for a short time
(c) own devices – inventing or making up things by yourself
(d) absently – in a faraway manner
5. (a) devices (b) absently (c) luxuries
(d) temporarily

Pages 21–24 No-one Special

A. 1. (b) 2. (e) 3. (a) 4. (b) 5. (c)

B. 1. Teacher check
2. (b) (e) (a) (c) (f) (d)
3. (a) snub (i) adjective; short, turned-up
(ii) snub can also be used as a verb – to rebuff or ignore.
(b) bear (i) verb; stand, or put up with.
(ii) bear can also be a noun – a large furry animal.
(c) lift (i) verb; raise up
(ii) lift can also be a noun – a machine which moves people up and down between floors.

Pages 25–28 Night Fright

A. 1. (d) 2. (b) 3. (c) 4. (d) 5. (b)

B. 1. Nocturnal means 'active at night' or similar wording
2. (d) (b) (h) (c) (g) (e) (a) (f)
3. Teacher check
4. (a) responsibility – a duty or care
(b) unsupervised – not in adult care, no overseer
(c) absorbed – soaked up, taken in
(d) determine – to settle in or decide
5. (a) unsupervised (b) responsibility, determine
(c) absorbed

Pages 29–33 The Date

A. 1. (c) 2. (a) 3. (a) 4. (d) 5. (b)

B. 1. (b) (c)
2. Teacher check
3. Teacher check
4. Teacher check
5. (a) luminous – giving off or reflecting light
(b) automatically – working or going by itself; like a machine
(c) anonymous – having no name given
(d) avoiding – keeping away from